Zen of Pop

poems

GEORGE GUIDA

Copyright © 2020 by George Guida

All rights reserved.

No part of this book may be reproduced or used in any format or by any means, electronic or mechanical, including photocopying, recording, scanning, or by any information storage and retrieval device or system, without prior written permission from the publisher.

Published in the United States by Long Sky Media, sending out signals from the island city of Alameda, California.

Find us online: LongSkyMedia.com

ISBN: 978-1-946588-04-3

Book and cover design by Helen Bruno

Printed in the United States of America

also by GEORGE GUIDA

New York and Other Lovers: Poems
(Revised Edition)

Pugilistic: Poems

Spectacles of Themselves:
Essays in Italian American Popular Culture and Literature

The Sleeping Gulf: Poems

The Pope Stories and Other Tales of Troubled Times

Low Italian: Poems

The Peasant and the Pen:
Men, Enterprise and the Recovery of Culture in
Italian American Narrative

ACKNOWLEDGMENTS

Earlier versions of the following poems appear in the following publications:

"Untitled, With Barry Manilow," and "You Outlive the King of Pop"—*Foundlings*

"Now Is That, Love?"—*Ghost City Review*

"Alec Baldwin's Ghost"—*Long Island Literary Journal*

"American Race Song" and "Baker Street"—*Long Island Quarterly*; reprinted in *Foundlings*

"Kiss the Girl"—*Maple Leaf Poetry VII: 40th Anniversary Issue*

"Elegy for a Beach Boy's Smile" (as "Elegy for Brian Wilson's Smile")—*Poet Sounds: An Anthology of Poems Inspired by the Beach Boys' Pet Sounds* (City Lit Press); reprinted in *Composing Poetry: A Guide to Writing Poetry and Thinking Lyrically.* (Kendall Hunt Press)

"B. A. Baracus," "Journey Inside a Russian Barbershop," and "What Seems Still Whirls"—*Poetry Hotel*

"Scarface"—*POST(blank)*

"Boom!"—*Valley Voices*

*"Guantanamera" was a semi-finalist for *The Tishman Review*'s 2019 Edna St. Vincent Millay Poetry Prize.

"Surrender, surrender,
but don't give yourself away."

—Cheap Trick

POEMS

Untitled, with Barry Manilow   1

ABBA and the Impact of Climate Change   3

Elegy for a Beach Boy's Smile   5

The Rumors about Donna Summer   7

Gone to Rehab   8

You Outlive the King of Pop   11

Moonwalk   12

Sly   13

American Race Song   14

Dwight   15

B. A. Baracus   18

Zen of Johnny Mathis   20

Garfunkel   22

Guantanamera   24

Rolling Stones Capuzzelle   26

Scarface   28

It's a Fine Afternoon for an Irish Band 29

Journey Inside a Russian Barbershop 30

∞

Pints 34

Hewlett Harbor 35

Now Is That, Love? 37

Where Are You, Heart? 39

Kiss the Girl 40

Not Your Girlfriend 42

Sarah Bernhardt! 44

The Gospel According to Aretha 46

If Dylan were a poem, he'd be 47

Maggie and the Horse 49

Kurt Cobain Fading Away 50

Baker Street 51

Married to What You Do 52

After making love you almost whisper 53

Beyond the Beatles Suite 54

John Lennon at the Dakota 54

Paul McCartney's Coin of the Realm   55

Ringo's the Gent Over There   56

George Harrison Died, Too.   57

∞

WOLFMAN JACK AND EVERYBODY ELSE   60

WHEN GYPSIES SETTLE DOWN   63

LEDBETTER   65

MACARTHUR PARK COVERED AGAIN   67

I BELIEVE THE CHILDREN   69

ALEC BALDWIN'S GHOST   70

THE AWKWARD OUTRAGE OF FRED GOLDMAN   72

THE IDIOSYNCRASY OF OTIS REDDING   74

BEING STEVIE WONDER   76

ZEN OF BRUCE LEE   77

A FOOL BELIEVES   78

WINTER 1944   79

WHAT SEEMS STILL WHIRLS   80

BOOM!   83

THE COLONEL DREAMS EQUESTRIAN ELVIS   84

Elvis Costello in the Bargain Bin   86

José Feliciano's National Anthem   88

Eubie's Rag   90

Louis Prima at the Carousel Bar   91

Nothing But Love Songs   93

A Mother Explains the Lyrics   94

Zen of Iggy Pop   96

Zen of Pop

Untitled, with Barry Manilow

I dream of Barry Manilow
singing in German: *Ich bin muzick,
und I write ze songs.* Ach!
I have freighted my life with snark.
Ich bin creature of a facile globe.
Why not move to Vegas?
where I'll watch him command
union-built proscenia.

When you sing for a living
you belong to a guild,
a medieval aegis for rising chords.
The progression of ages
launches the son of Ashkenazi Jews
into the Golden Age of Disco.

Ballads, you say, are passé.
Ech! *Ist du taub?*
I wish I spoke German
instead of mocking it.
You pronounce it *Man-ee-love*:
Polish, Russian. Who knows
which nation to vanquish
or who wrote which song,
what love he gave or why?

A man under Bette Midler's spell
won't question the spheres.
He accepts what he hears
as common call. I wish I had
a doppelganger far enough away
who sang and dreamt the way
a doppelganger does. For Barry
it was Tony, who loved Lola,
once a showgirl, many songs ago.
I have never had a show
the world would want to see,

but I own a white tuxedo.
The clothes and eyes should speak
two tongues at once, should meet
the people who never knew
top forty. Is that too large
a herd of ears headed for
the monstrous maw? Barry is Mol-
och! His crimped skin claims
absolute authorship:
Ich bin muzick!
What if Beethoven crooned
that tune to Kant?

If I were *Man-ee-love* I'd say
I am not music. *Ich nicht bin.*
I'd say I can hear it, though.
Ich nicht bin Man-ee-love.
I'd say we crave a single voice,
but I am, you see, the thing
the music wishes it could be.

ABBA and the Impact of Climate Change

Winter in Stockholm means snuggle up and sing.
So do spring, summer and fall. Falling in love
to song will fix the fates of singers above
the latitude where ice is neverending.

If it had been a warmer place, Benny and Bjorn would not
have flown to Cyprus for a break, with Anni-Frid
and Agnetha, to play for U. N. troops in need
of a party, to become engaged, *festfolket*.

Melodifestivalen in any language
means hits with melodies you can't escape.
At best these numbers would have been shrouds draped
over wounds, "Waterloo" a scene of musical carnage,

the product of temperate marriage and climatic ennui,
Only the perpetually cold can yearn for something in the air,
for a sweaty dancing king or queen with feathered hair,
for a mama mia to ring a bell, for a hot-blooded *bon ami*.

With a hotter atmosphere and higher sea levels
ABBA's ship of music would have dropped a different anchor.
A thousand-year drought would have starved Ravi Shankar
and a flood would have drowned every one of the Nevilles,

Bob Marley would have fled the rising tides for Tennessee
and written country reggae songs with Dolly Parton,
who, with his encouragement, would have set her heart on
a joint tour to benefit the overwhelmed West Indies,

the Beach Boys would have taken to a bluff,
would have picked up banjos, bodhráns, flutes and bouzoukis,
and inspired by the view, written step dance riffs with harmonies
in Gaelic, driving the public to declare, "Enough!"

Woody Guthrie would have written so many dust bowl ballads
that farmers would have told him to give it a rest,
while Mideast immigrants to the New Midwest
would sit today in Main Street cafes that serve tabbouleh salads,

teaching the locals the lore of their musical heroes—
Fairuz, Umm Kulthum, Asmahan, Abedel Halim Hafez—
conquering landscapes of heartland sound as if Cortés
had come to Columbus, or La Salle returned to Chicago,

waves of migration would have swept Youssou N'Dour
to the throne of Anglophone pop, his musical equation
borrowing tones from the Arctic Invasion,
which carries us back to ABBA's door,

once closed by, you could say, life on the road,
but I'd say more by changes in median temperature.
The world that drew them became a shrinking aperture
that darkened the dawn of those shivery, shimmery odes,

which might have melted away like time
were it not for a Hollywood crew and the dross
they produced on the doomed Greek isle of Skopelos,
numbers and plot that may as well have been mime.

Ten years later they've promised to return as avatars,
smooth-skinned holograms immune to climate change
and death, projected onto a looming sea or mountain range,
singing songs that will have been written on Mars.

Elegy for a Beach Boy's Smile

```
If Brian Wilson can't be happy
                                        how can I?
When a boy of summer cries,
                         how can I
be Loki to Thor?
                       How can sounds be mine?
Can I be sound's?
                       Be happy I was?— or wasn't
his order, or any
                       or sky?


Or try it this way
                       with more with more
cherubs as castrati,
                       cellos, celestial saws

                       to

let me go home.
                       I feel so, you know,
let me go,
                       whatever you are,
my brother singing,
                            Linus reining lions,
stripes on small-screen shirts
                            flying mini-skirts on stage,
burning surfboards
                       on doo-wop sand,
descending ego,
                     ignoring war,
             and if God only knew
                                     why did only Carl sing?
```

And if Mike Love
                        could never love
how can I
                be love, be nice, be loved?
Love can't be.
                    I have no books or poetry.
Just cap and beard
                    protect me, no Apollo
to burn the tempo,
                    to burnish these times.

If you ask, my answer
                    is a girl set free,
Ra humming so loud
                    you split your skin,
feel it break, so broke up,
                          every time so broke
up, so broken
                the double horn declares
that's not,
            that can't,
                      just won't be me.

The Rumors about Donna Summer

she was a drag queen (like you) yet Christian all the way (like you)
hated gays, called AIDS a divine plague (like you) died of AIDS spoke
German married a German man although she was a man (like you)
had Nazi sympathies (like you) she was black (like you) was really a
white man (like you) took the name Summer (like you) because it
sounded better than Spring wrote to forget (like you) the child she
could never have   because she was like you

what if you are a rumor? or nothing (like you)? what if you can't
dance? they said she couldn't, but she did you are not who you say she
was you didn't do what she thought she did disco never happened
why can't we all be Donna Summer? we are beautiful we can all
write hits can all be 17-minute songs We are woman and man,
remembered and forgotten the rumor we hear is ourselves,
you are and death (like you) dies (like you)
when she sings a song (you heard) she never wanted to

Gone to Rehab

I am. Out of black, you'd say.
Yes, ironic. Not the rehab.
A song's a song.
I mean me liking it,
cause when I started coming
it was like going to a gym.
I just, you know, built it
into schedule, did the reps.
Then it came natural,
like a beat, That's why
I stayed where I can sit
and think. Sometimes I write.
That's the only way
the good can come.
The crap sort of sorts itself.
I used to be happy
writing songs about weed,
about being in love,
but I'm not anymore,
not in love. Love makes you
like a bomb. That's what
the doctors don't say,
but I figured it out.
From being in here.
I figured I could write
about whatever. Like
being maternal.
I am. My friends call me
"Mum without the damage."
I still have friends.
They want me out, say,
"Enough's enough, right?"
But I just say no, no
and no. It's easy here.
And you know what pays
the monthly bill? Right,
that song. And my dad.
When I sang about my daddy,
I didn't mean some sugar.
He was good. I was naughty.
A naughty little girl,

but not with tantrums.
I just played my tune.
How I wanted to be
a waitress when I was young,
before the music, before I listened
to, like, MoTown, and black girls
singing, and I thought
if I wasn't a Jew,
what they wanted me to be,
I'd be black. I'd be anything
the white world could love
and hate the same. So
I'd thank my audience
and tell them all sod off.
All fake, and me a phony
my family wouldn't recognize,
though they wanted me
to wear disguises.

Regret anything? Why?
I'm young. Still young,
though in the world
I'm old as memory.
Christ, that sounds like
some philosophy.
It boils down to being
glad I didn't marry
my boyfriend Ray
or the other one
and become a housewife
who sings in the kitchen
when no one wants to hear
the songs she knows. Here
I sing them wherever,
whenever I want, and a lot
of the types who live here
are too far gone to say
shut up, stop the noise, keep it
to yourself, you bloody tart.
So I sing. Even the odd
Madonna song. Yeah.

I do regret we never met
or did a number or had a row.
I called her to visit,
but she said she was busy,
said I'm depressed,
what the doctors say
But what does it mean
when Madonna and doctors agree?
You ask me, the world's depressed.
But that's living, listening
to what people have to say,
to what they want to sing.
Tony Bennett knows.
Granddad, I call him. Yeah,
sometimes he comes.
We sit on the verandah.
Sometimes he comes with groceries,
and we commandeer the kitchen,
cook Italian food all day.
Sometimes we have a drink,
like we were on a cruise
though, of course, without
the vino and the view.
So, you know, it might be
just a cup of tea
while he tells me stories,
the world in 1959
and what it's like today.
We lean back in our chairs
and laugh until we cry
and then when they turn out the lights
we cuddle on the couch
and sing each other lullabies.

You Outlive the King of Pop

He glides across the screen,
mimes your will to conquer fear,
as much a child as you were then,
even if that year you turned nineteen.

When next you hear him sing, he is a man
and you are balding, as he shakes himself
down to dance floors you never owned
but knew would exist to slide across.

Apotheosis takes you by surprise,
but makes more sense when he appears,
battle-sequined, full enigma now. The world
broadcasts his voice in every public space.

Decline is nothing you don't expect.
He's easy to forget as any life you've left.
His voice recedes to zen of pop, returns
at weddings where you moonwalk frowns.

Death arrives when you no longer care
to ponder hues. His woo-hoos limelight
a final scene: masses screaming
in flight from a stage on artificial fire.

A little child is not supposed to die
while singing of love gone wrong.
His absent dance does right for someone else
who thought he knew the moves he couldn't do.

Moonwalk

Poor Michael Jackson,
always gliding backward to
a lunar childhood.

Sly

Man, imagine what I'm dealing with.
First, Stallone takes my name,
then Prince shows up.
So I'm a man in a comfortable cave,
a century of names that time forgot.
I'm the man before the man,
the sun that goes down and comes up
on another planet. He's gone, I'm here,
and I'll tell you the lyrics,
but I'm too hoarse to sing.
That's why I sold my songs.
I have too much.
The money will never run out
if you respect the business
and the business man.
Money is nothing
Mohammad Ali and I
spoke about money and rights
and animosity. We agreed
on the power of words, but
he tried to say that black folks
could take their words away
and live in a separate country.
Go ahead, Mohammad, stand,
build a country in the sky, but
we've got to live together.
You can't separate the groups.
If we did that there'd be no Prince,
you dig? And what became of them
when they walked among us?
Ambassadors to the world.
Still, Mohammad had a point.
We—black people, I'm saying—
are like me—the man behind
the Man. We built all this just like
I built grooves that people paid
real scratch to hear, that people paid
their wages to own. And when I say
people, I mean everyday people
and Michael Jackson.

American Race Song

Something's wrong with your soul
if it won't swoon when Sam Cooke sings,
It's been too hard livin', but I'm afraid.
And when you hear it I hope you think
of dogs and how they can't see shades
and if for this they are beloved
of those who light the lamps that line
the blood procession's route.

The side your skin is on depends
on the day your papa had
when you were ten, his words
for colors who cut him off and left
you three score years to think of them
as *them* who'd knock you on your knees
as soon as take your hand.

You will have to last too long
to drink the breath and sweat
of love that lingers in your throat
like dust of a planet you never see
on nights when you leave the little tent
by a river that used to be time
to understand how natives spoke
the night before they sent
their painted parties out
to greet horizon's dots and dance
the rhythms of distant smoke.

Dwight

I don't own the clothes I'm wearing.
I'll just return them to the earth

like silver to mine and
mind to natural turn,

that rainbow riverbend
where posses ride from sight.

Drop the guitar.
Pick up the badge.

Leave by moonlight.
Let frets and pearling gleam.

I, Bandit, pinned note to door,
lit out for badlands,

traded spangles for blues,
blended into sky. Divine

intervention, I swear. The Lord
slipped me bullets for the day

Mama said to never let
any fool kill you twice.

Mama knew. She caught
the gleam in Daddy's eyes.

When you ask for the license
watch the tail lights' pulse.

When you leave a perp to die
in the desert, rattlers rise.

If the body's decided
they slither away.

*I ride Boulevards of Death
through Neighborhoods of Doom.*

That's a little joke we have,
but sometimes I don't laugh.

Sometimes I sing,
to jangle invisible coins.

One's an old-time silver dollar
for moments of denial.

Most of this is true except
I never knew the suspect's name

or that we sat in once
on the same small stage.

I have no right to pose,
to sunglasses when I play.

I wish I could croon
to the hands of a clock,

wish I could shoot to maim
progressions of time.

The songs are no more
white or black than you.

It's the measures and sounds
in the rumble and rhythm

that keeps the moonlight blue
and the badge in the glove.

This piece right here
is an act of love

and you'll see it that way.
This is how I sacrifice

a lifetime roaming streets,
cuffing the hands of misery

to keep them from your doors.
I trace circles on the bar

as outlaws, targets
for the beads we draw.

Here's what you hear:
Crimes burn criminals

and we trade sins
for a President's silver skull.

B. A. Baracus

Palm Sunday as prelude to pietà.
A lector reads the Gospel of Barrabas
while I fold my cross and think *B. A.
Barrabas*, flubbing a namesake scholars say
may have been Jesus himself, the son
of a father, like Mr. T's, absconded.

Mohawk, a kinky antenna to channel
four centuries' whips. B. A. for Bad
Attitude, which he had, and ratings
and a movie role to bloody White Hope
who spoke Italian Philly, language
only half as old as a new world self.

Baldness bespoke Clean as much as T
if you were inclined to shine the token,
if you bought the hype. For a while he was
the hype, as they used to say. Baracus
had no pity, had no mercy for the fool
who, in casting, set him only half-way free.

They called him John Henry, Stepin Fetchit,
a thick-necked Tom on his own golden leash
but the country preferred his muscled grunts
to blood-witted, hatchet-tongued black men
fated to spray misshapen topiary
with history's holy water cannon.

Self-baptized Mandinka Igbo guarding
ten clothes designers, twenty-nine celebrities
twelve models, fifteen judges, and forty millionaires,
Laurence T. Tereud charged three grand a night,
if you could get him and his jewelry and his
two hundred law-suited tussles in tow.

He chewed and spit those numbers through his teeth,
through grins at wrestlers and President's wives
planted on mats and laps as gifted gaffes.
He chopped the forests of Chicagoland,
Paul Bunyan and ox, shedding chains
like qualms about playing a self to death.

Then came the Flood, absolving him of gold,
cartooning him for screens, aggrieving him
in the name of all those who've suffered
the cruelties of fiction on pedestals.
Barrabas, Baracus, human abacus
on the altar figuring all of us.

Zen of Johnny Mathis

Rubato and vibrato,
the smooth pyrotechnics
of galaxies

a-swirl in a flute
set by a fire
built for ecstasy.

Addiction to champagne,
the wage of sweetness
and philosophy:

Be the fluid
in the fingerbowl.
Be the agency.

Be the athlete
until music and mentors
show you how the body

can be your instrument
and your business.
"Homosexuality

is a lifestyle I've grown
accustomed to," he came
to admit, breezily.

As though his vaulting
were a secret, or his distaste
for controversy.

How high a man may leap
only leaving leaping
helps him see.

Sprung from mixed race
Texas stock into
Mitch Miller's goatee,

led by the hand for his gifts
to a tree where love
demands high Es,

he picked the ripest apples,
whose crimson sheen
was melody,

decided he was
everything and nothing,
in a symphony,

so an orchestra follows
him and will through
soundtracks and eternity.

But he does not swell
with strings or rumble
with tympany.

He sings. He is
celestial before
and after he dies. Free.

Garfunkel

Yo, Man, whatchu listenin' to?
Garfunkel? he asked as I
walked the subway platform.
Couldn't possibly be
James Brown. My style:
long curly hair, long nose,
thin, with yellow Walkman,
black tee shirt New Yorker
adrift in the 1980s.
The last thing I wanted
was for anyone to think
my music was too white.
A black man thinking it,
even worse, the shame
of privilege unsung as such,
the knowledge of whiteness,
a family story we all believed
but knew in private music
of our thoughts to be a lie.

I was meant to believe,
having come from blackness,
had heard the beats, the hip,
the hop, was truly a child
of integrated schools
(unintegrated towns)
so of course Paul Simon
came from Queens, the borough
once white as folksy harmonies
and Garfunkel's voice,
never mind the bridge
over trouble. That was fake
church. One of many
appropriations. *Derivative*,
slur, no homage in theft
until you understood
how growing older made a man
less himself and more a human
being. African and South
American names I'd never seen
heard over and over began

to sound like the rhythm
of feelings I'd had since
before I could remember.

Garfunkel believed in himself
and for this the world
has forgotten he existed
without Simon, has made him
the butt of a joke that only
someone who believes in whiteness
would get. His hair is curly,
Simon's is gone, and mine
is straight as a walk through time
to a night on the Great Lawn,
when Simon is playing solo
with a global cast, and I
sit there, still young, with a love
I'd leave behind, and think
this is why I love New York,
a city I've lost just as sure
as streaming music killed
the Walkman and made Simon
another fortune, and maybe
Garfunkel too. Maybe Garfunkel
remembers feeling himself
too cool and yet so white
that he feared that black man's
question as though music
would always make him
something he was not.

Guantanamera

I'm no Cuban, but I hang with Juan,
Puerto Rican by way of Queens,
who, after years of research, wrote
of a *tío's* time playing rumba and *son*.
Juan hears Babalú-Ayé
in calls and horns. He knows orishas
from Congo gods and tells me
Desi Arnaz was ersatz, his word,
how his father, Desiderio,
while *alcalde* of Santiago,
banned the conga, then fled his home
for Florida, to raise a son
destined to suffer at Lucy's hands.

Cuban *son* is music played
by a sestet featuring a *tres*.
Polyrhythm and simple math,
but have you ever thought
while driving along the shore,
radio booming, I need to hear
some *son*? Yet there it is,
to drive "Guantanamera,"
and all the earworms hatched
from centuries of pain,
survival, migration,
the cane and distant shore.

"Guantanamera" is a patriotic song
with lyrics by a poet soon to die,
a sincere man sharing his soul
before he goes. Juan and I also are
sincere men but our souls
are not Guantanameros.
How could they be
with what's happened there
in the life of the dead *guajira?*
How could they be
when we take what we want
from her country and pain, and sing
as if bound by sin to dance?

Juan and I try the singer's song,
growing roses for friends, and shame
for bondage, love for the poor.
We've listened well, to share good cries
about mankind and the limits of art.
We walk the streets of winter,
clacking claves in our heads,
willing ourselves to do the steps.
though the *guajira* never sees.
We console ourselves with visions
of her hip sway by a mountain stream
whose water we love as much
as the beat of the ocean between.

Rolling Stones Capuzzelle

Sometimes I wish for '73
when I took family traits
like plates of *capuzzelle*,
and set them to a 12-string blues,
a string for each Epiphany,
a blues-ell crescendo
wailing me to sleep
in a dago burg that raised
the goats for spells to cast
like dice against a bayou
portiere a hundred years ago
settled like silt, and risen
with the rap of a snare,
no more walled by *zias*' arms.
I was a bell-bottom, glassed-in fool
a man, a boy, behind a veil,
abandoned mandolin
rejiggered for arpeggios.

Demons boiled to eyes and tongue
in the Church of the Bad Guitar.
One morning I left the manger
to worship and return
through light a star,
an Anglophile star,
an un-Latin you, a name
like a year that never existed
in old world time. I was the new
winter of Sunday dinner
and Mr. D of prayer
to safer gods and sepia hearts
in chords that overpowered
calls from feudal fields
whose heartbreak harvest
is a string of breezy Doooos.

Fair-haired for once I rode
a golden train, and spooned
a meal from a silk-screened can,
chewed my *capuzzelle*
wide-mouthed. Goatskinned,

I must have been dreaming
variations on a theme
in backing vocals:
Mick and David Bowie,
Mick and Ronnie Wood,
Mick and Ida Verdi
on a Campania farm.
As I rode away I would have
fallen in love, as Mick had tried
with his mother's lips,
and father's tongue,
and fingertips playing
an olden phrase thieved
from a sonata, but
in '73 I couldn't wanna.

Scarface

The night Tony Montana died—
a thousand bullets and a balcony plunge
face-first into an indoor fountain—
Johnny Farrell next to me down front
stood up and yelled, *Shoot him again,
drive him to the bottom.*

We hadn't yet gone our separate ways.
Johnny still trusted me enough
to call the special ed playground Tardo Park.
I wasn't a teacher then, and he was my best friend
that year, the kid I most wanted to be:
good looking, tough, in that Irish way.

We plated weights and walked the town,
fifteen-and-a-half in tight jeans and tees,
as girls would yell from passing cars
but never stop to talk. Good.
Our mouths spat blanks. We bled
ketchup through phony get-ups.

Johnny told the biggest guy in school
he wished he had his size. If only, what'd he do.
Then laughed at the lack. I tried
not to suspend disbelief. Not Johnny,
who swore to Pacino's fall, so I now see
my gangster corpse still floating there.

It's a Fine Afternoon for an Irish Band

like the Pogues, for instance, if you'll recall them
and you're the kind who's off on Fridays
spinning old vinyl and thinking of strife
in the world and its menace to home sweet home,
spinning theory from problems of fact.

At least your friends share taste in song,
for the growling singer and the fife and drum.
The growling is wrong too hard to feel, the accent
is lives destroyed by brutal marauders.
What if the reel played hunger in blood?

What if you knew the Irish drum's name?
At least you remember the Chieftains,
overweight as this latest you,
in kilts on your childhood screen,
less Irish than what you imagine.

So recall a lass as Celtic as
the wife disappeared in Sligo's map
all over your grown son's face as he drops
the needle to all the unfaithful departed,
their keening that works a familiar hook.

Journey Inside a Russian Barbershop

When Yuriy parts my hair
he chuckles at some demon in his ear.
Boris, at the other chair,
responds in Russian with a frown.
He is saying these Americans
are fools to come to us
who learned to barber hair
between attacks in Chechnya
and threats of execution.

Or they speak in their language
of the music that blares
from speakers behind the screen
where the underworld plays in loops.
Boris says that Journey's singer
intones with the power of a Czar's
Budyonnies. Yuriy remarks
that he wails like a waif
suffering at Putin's hands.

Everything around the shop
is just what you'd expect:
the jars of Mane 'n Tail,
aristocrat of Clubman talc
on shelves above the fade and trim
electric clippers dangling
from the hooks by tight arrays
of silver shears the mirror casts
as bazar of ego stokes
only these two can wield
as secrets they use
to keep each other in line.

Yuriy says no, my hair should never be
so long. "Has it been six months?"
Boris shrugs and juts his lip,
the same as when his wife might ask
what he'll do about their son,
the American, who is ashamed of them
and won't wake up on time for school,
and lies he doesn't smoke

when of course they know
his tee shirts reek like workers'
bars in Niszhny Novgorod.

His is also the lip to know
how gray the hair is falling
on my lap and how when I talk
about my latest scan, he might well say
"You know, we all hang by a thread,"
and how at another immigrant shop
I watched my father's strands of hair
fall to the floor like all small deaths,
from chairs of foreigners
whose tongue he wished he knew.

For a time I believed I'd learn
Russian, to read the classics
because the soul resides in a crone,
her smile, and a clerk, his rants.
But I'm thankful Yuri's learned
the English of this trade.
He waves a straight-edge, searching
for words to conceal my gray,
then yells "Dye!" as failure he knows
I don't have courage to regret
mocks me with the curse of those
whose hair grows in the grave.

When he asks what color I prefer
I mean to answer brown,
but thinking it's too late
tell him let it be.
Boris runs thick fingers
through his midnight mop
as though tonics could preserve
the flesh the way the tundra does.
I want to remind them how
the winter chills with wasted chances,
blizzards teach us to spend ourselves,
and icicles linger like stubborn hair
no one but nature can cut.

And the band born long ago
near the Russian River Valley
plays another song insisting
we believe that we belong
somewhere. "Yuriy, we are lost,"
I almost say, but his eyes have found
the mirror where a stallion in a meadow
brays at the lullabies and strokes
of a dead babushka's warming hand.

Pints

Rod Stewart downed a few
aboard his private plane.
We wouldn't have called it ale,
still too young to drink
anything but Buds in cans
our older cousins muled us
from convenience stores.

The story spread that
Rod had drunk a pint of scum.
We meant sperm or cum
but called it scum, because
he was dirty, prowling
stages in leather pants.

Thirty years later a mate
called him "tart" for leaving,
going solo for a fame
that made us care
when doctors pumped his stomach
and flushed a pint of scum

How it got there no one knew.
None of us had done those deeds,
put the ball in the back of the net,
as they said in the Highgate
low-life tongue of his youth.
None of us spoke of uncles
touching us or how we pulled
a sad girl's panties down.
Scum flushed blood and tears.

We whispered the rumor
behind our school, went home
to see him slither into disco,
exposing shoulders, winking
at sins we hid from
parents in next-room pajamas
who toasted what we'd become.

Hewlett Harbor
for John

The lightless streets of Hewlett Harbor
were moats between mansions and us.

You called them mansions. You said, *Ask me
if I care?* and waited for an answer

as you disappeared from school, let stubble grow,
rolled packs of smokes in tee shirt sleeves.

You turned the headlights off and hit the gas,
slammed the gate at eighty-five. Born again

to speed, you laughed the way you could
those Friday nights of our spinning disks,

our launching from a couch, to smash
our air guitars, the way boys did.

Speed erased our fallings out,
Gs pulled us close two ways.

Our fathers' voices—grumbles, songs—
glued hands to wheel, pressed feet to floor

as we listened to them singing
duets in the darkened road.

What played on the eight-track I couldn't say,
except that notes of freedom filled our ears.

You spent your life taking men to jail
while I did my part to keep them out

neither of us knowing right.
So I jumped in when you passed

and you never hit the brakes until
the word that somehow you were gone.

You drove with, not through, the night.
Neither of us saw that far ahead.

The glow of mansion windows dimmed our eyes,
so we thought to share a dream

but never took that turn. Instead,
if you believe in souls, we prayed

through power chords to understand
all that we'd been missing in the light.

Now Is That, Love?

      My high school girlfriend,
                       so Eighties Cool
                       she unveiled tofu
                       in her fridge
                       to say
                It lives in water

                                   ordered me
                                   sushi in a new
                                   resutoran
                                   Indian-styling
                                   on her tatami.

In her bedroom of posterless walls
                       she heckled
                       makeup and lace

          screened me

                                   "Repo Man"
                                   and loved that
                                   nobody cared

       coaxed images
       from toxic darkroom baths

                                   because she didn't want to live
                                   past fifty-nine

       shot burnouts
       in parking lots and snotty
       little sisters flipping birds

                                   mailed them
                                   to kids we knew

                                   letters addressed to names
                                   that sounded like their names
                  if you were stoned

                                        letters threatening lawsuits
                                        unless they would admit
                      their links to the accused.

She gifted me a photo:
herself with cat in arms
which I drew the best I could

                                    and handed her the sketch
                                    before the final bell.

She may have believed me
when once or twice I said

                    I loved her
                    so she bent my finger
                    back, and asked
                    Now is that love?

            and did it again
            the year we met grown up
            with houses and spouses
            and sons and daughters,
            a Squeeze song playing
            in both our heads

                    and I asked her
                    as she pushed a little harder,
                    Now, Love, don't you know?

Where Are You, Heart?

See the child *bailarina del vientre* on a table mothers set,
on migration's winds from Lebanon, from Iberia's pulse,
in a country foreign as the word "vibrato." The nun sneered,
You sound like a goat, and she thinks only of Armero,
goats on hillsides, plummeting landslides, goats as alarms
in a storm, and people who never hear them. Tragedy
she would play, the tragedy of those who never hear the words
their hearts can't sing to them until hearts give way to hips
and we repeat the lies, about exotic dances and curves,
of how a lover's figure rescues us from tortures of true loves
who fail to love us in our rhythm. Simply, she is fiction of amor.

How your ringtone drew me in with promises of bliss. It was she
(was her) you wanted me to hear, this "singer/songwriter/dancer/
record producer/businesswoman/philanthropist/actress/model/
goodwill ambassador" to the Top 40, as siren I would never have
to leave, as you. The truth is that you both wrote poems once
before you saw the world and how its women, immigrants, fools
too often end in silence. I think of you writing those poems on a shore
remote as the day we met in Wyclef's Jean's faux tropics,
singing *Shakira, Shakira*, as faux as the claim he never knew
she could dance like this. Really, how hard can Spanish be to learn
when you sing someone else's song as though it were your own?

Kiss the Girl

I dread the play the way I love the tale
of a college friend who gained his fame
by being obsessed with Ariel. Obsessed
with a cartoon, this guy who said things
so crude about women they made even us
barbaric young men leave the table.

How his dorm-room answering machine announced
that he and the Little Mermaid were out, but
if you left a message, they'd call you back.
His mother calling, hearing, saying, *Fuck you,
and Fuck the Little Mermaid!* His roommate
forwarding the message campus wide.

How years later I was making coffee
in an apartment shared with my first wife
and switched the radio on and heard
his mother cursing both of them
and then the radio host explaining how
my friend was living off his legend.

I dread the high school musical version
in the auditorium where I starred
years before my sophomore niece was born.
But we come back every year, my family—
second wife, son, sisters, cousins, in-laws—
the way the vaguely Catholic go to Easter mass.

To prepare myself, I think about desserts
my sister will have waiting at her house.
The after-party as mother to the ritual.
The party I left to drive to the beach
with a carload of friends and the girl I was sure
I'd marry if only she'd agree to a kiss.

The lights dim, the overture, and then
it happens. Ariel sings and I choke up.
Her voice is not the best, but she is poised,
the way we also were, because this struggling school
has always taken pride in a couple of things:
its theater and diversity.

The beautiful brown-skinned lead
and children of all races rise together
to the level of professionals and blood,
loving one another as the audience does
for their harmonies and steps, for how
they show us in song what to be.

I believe I'm fighting back tears because
I believe it was my generation
who finally took equality on faith.
It was we who showed the world
how we could gain ourselves
by sharing souls for all to see.

My eyes are watery, my voice cracking
as my biracial niece, who's just declared
herself my nephew, takes a curtain call.
We rise to our feet, until the cast descends
into the aisles and familiar arms,
and I want, as I did last year, to tell the actors

how years ago I stood up there, how proud
I am of them and what they've done.
But I decide that act is old, and better to leave
the moment theirs. Instead I walk my elderly father
to the doors, then head alone to the car,
dodging children playing in cool night air.

What a beautiful scene it is, but as I walk
I begin to cry again, because I'm following
an old route home from school,
understanding how reckless I've been
to cherish scenes that don't replace
a love we didn't need to recall.

Not Your Girlfriend
after Amorak Huey

Far as we could tell, Joan Jett was no one's girlfriend.
A ninth-grade buddy told me he'd found out
she lived on a golf course one town over,
no shock she lived so close, the way she acted
like so many Long Island girls we knew.
Their lips like soft fangs, they could take you
or leave you. But on a golf course?
Was I supposed to imagine her
gathering pine cones from the rough
to make Christmas wreaths for neighbors' doors?
She had to be lighting the cones on fire,
hurling them at civil lawyers on the fairway.
But that was before I knew how she felt
about animal rights, about helping the creatures
who'd limp by her door, struck by golf balls,
the helpless ones the men in argyle ignored.
Joan was keeping her enemies closer.

She was tough as the girl who lived next door,
whose brothers used to knock each other senseless,
yell so loud my father, a cop, called the cops.
By rights that girl should have blasted her music,
but instead she smiled when she left for school
and left it at hello. She was the perfect girlfriend,
if you liked your girlfriends imaginary.
At fourteen I felt like I had no choice, but I did
have the choice of whom to imagine. Joan Jett
didn't make the list. It was clear she was no one's
fantasy, because it was clear she didn't need
a boyfriend's kiss to take the stage,
clear that she lied when she sang
about hating herself for loving you.
Joan Jett screamed *I'm not your girlfriend,*
I don't want to touch you, and
I'll never be your cherry bomb.

The issue now is what Joan Jett knew
and how she came to know it.
I think about boys and men,
how they behaved when I was young
and how a lot still do, and I think about Joan
and her family, about how they moved around
and how they split, and how she took
her mother's maiden name and used it
to conquer rock 'n roll, and how she meets
with Cherrie Currie now and then
at some Long Island diner, to laugh
at the grown men who came to drool
at an underage lingerie girl with a mic,
how she and Cherrie have drinks at her house,
watch the foursomes chase their errant shots
remember seventeen, three power chords,
and lives' worth of better things to do.

Sarah Bernhardt!

She sleeps in a coffin
with a fresh bouquet
at my mother's wake.
In her kitchen I performed
tantrums and pleas.
Sarah Bernhardt!
If I overacted,
Sarah Heartburn!
My mother directed. *Cut
the crap*, she called
once the curtain fell.

Today again I am
the French actress,
involuntarily, because
living is involuntary.
Even my mother was only
partly responsible for my life
busy as she was
with the roles of page,
ingenue, nursemaid,
seductress, flower,
martyr, prince of Denmark.

The stage is set
and Sarah appears
as the mother
because the mother is
the role of mother
and also, at least once,
courtesan, and now
idol on an altar.
The mother foretells her demise
and so mine's died
ten tragedies' worth of deaths
before this final scene.

In turn I rely on DNA
and preparation
and my place on stage
for this latest performance
of a grief that comes
as naturally as the tears
of la Divine, the starstruck child.

The Gospel According to Aretha

Her Afro is a nimbus, her voice is liquid soul spilled verse by verse on sacred scrolls.

Have you ever loved a woman with a direct line to God, whatever you call her in the dark, with the radio on by your side as though she were lying next to you, your cool-skinned lover at dawn who whispers the worries she doesn't sing?

Don't confuse worries with troubles. Don't confuse this woman always there for a prayer.

She is more a story that never quite gets told but saves itself up for stage shouts, for more audience than you can ever be.

She belongs to everyone with ears that ring with b-flat melodies and ecstasies of sensual saints.

Even as you touch her tender, sloping shoulder you will only ever know her as supernatural.

Even if you live as Reverend Minister you will come to her blind until she sings a single miracle never twice the same.

You will find her in the ether of Los Angeles, Las Cruces or Santa Fe, or further back in Saint Louis, Philadelphia, Detroit, or on the wings of Atalanta.

Her voice reminds you what you knew but couldn't speak: Time has always been a lie, but you are its shepherd until you die.

Think. Say a little prayer. Do these things in her wake, in her memory, and she will grant you peace if she feels it, and something like the music of eternity.

If Dylan were a poem, he'd be

not a poem but a word in spite of itself,
in spite of you but not out of spite, just out
for a good time in a sad way, or seeming to say
that one of his words would be something like "lout"
the medieval set on a pine wood shelf.

several forms and no form at all, verse as free
as taking notes and putting them in order,
as painting a face to make it replace
a thought you had and released in a chord
or a poem by way of Calliope.

nothing you'd recognize as such,
because songs aren't songs until
you sing them and not as dumb as words
a man might spit from a graphite quill.
Don't muffle your voice in clutches.

something other than a drug or spell.
He would tell you to be your own
iconoclast and then refuse bombastically
to answer a simple question like
How was it? How was what? He'd kvell.

the line that no one cares about poems
except poets who would be troubadours
without guitars or audience or scimitars
to slay the demons they want rumors
to say haunt them, poured out in requiem.

Joni Mitchell or Scarlet Rivera's violin,
with a touch of aging Ginsberg at the grave
of Kerouac, and a line of white and black
back-up singers who would save him
from having to talk to Roger McGuinn.

a shred of parchment paper as palimpsest
blown down a lonely street in Juárez
on the Day of the Dead or instead
fed to the flames by a seer in a fez
at Saint Maries de la Mer for the Gypsy fest.

an epic injustice never set right, a stream
of language threatening to turn inward
in a quest for genius and the rest
of nothing and knights who turn sinward
on a steed that outruns a dream.

regularly irregular and when
you least expected it he'd end.

Maggie and the Horse

By the time he opened Maggie and the Horse, Stephen had stopped believing in rare diseases. First his child vanished, then his wife built a fence, the kind James Taylor put up to keep out Carly Simon. Stephen played James Taylor songs on a loop. For years I went and listened to his songs, saw Stephen's family photos on the walls, and watched the owner prowl the dining room, asking me and everyone, *How's it taste?* before his sad face floated back behind the register. He told me he lived upstairs, and named the place for dogs who had the run, who lived through my whole first marriage, but didn't see the next. James Taylor persevered. Stephen installed new speakers and added a deck so everyone could hear. I asked if he'd get another dog or two. He shook his head and turned the music up. Then one day, when my new wife and I drove in, the place was closed, the tables gone, the walls bare, and Stephen vanished. On our way to the car, we heard the strum of a guitar and heard a voice from Stephen's window, singing about a simple twist of fate. In the middle of the refrain, the voice gave out, and I recalled James Taylor used to have a dog named Hercules.

Kurt Cobain Fading Away

Kurt wouldn't be loving the second half either.
Less time crunching chords and smashing Strats.
Garage for recycle bins, not band practice.
Landscapers waving from the lawn.

He would be signing old CDs for local cops.
Daughter with the mantel of junkie queen.
Her bail like a charge from Amazon.
His signature pasta dish the hit of Friday night.

Baker Street

You finally woke up
in that quiet little town,

threw on jeans and a short-sleeve shirt,
hopped in a car with a broken radio,

cruised down main street, because
you remembered how cool it was

to cruise, and blew your trumpet
out the driver's side window

at somebody like you
on one of those crazy days

stirred by in the breeze
like cobwebs above a bed

where you used to dream
about buying some land.

You blew the melody
you imagined you'd play

on that imaginary porch,
with chickens and children

wailing on the lawn
instead of an angry guitar.

Married to What You Do

J-Lo designed a line of coats.
        one of which my now-wife bought
the year that A-Rod won the Series.

Beyoncé sang "Single Ladies" right after
        I left my first wife for reasons
a man like Jay-Z could easily understand.

The world began to pretend
        Taylor Swift was a genius
when they got tired of Kanye.

Eminem doesn't like being married,
        which helps him because
he makes a living saying so.

Pink is always thinking about
        her husband, but never
sings his praises as a way to party.

Will Smith used to rap, but then
        he met the camera
and Jada Pinkett and luxury.

We are all married to the lens
        but cheat on it now and then
by beat-boxing to flesh and bone.

After making love you almost whisper

a sentence I almost understand, your still-
blond hair tangling my eyes, but you are no less
the goddess whose jug of wine is full when we
come into the world, when you sit up and say
I like spending time with you, and I remember
the Stones on the Ed Sullivan Show,
maybe the year we were born. Not to be
snide, but your wetness is witness
to time we've stolen from our child
and our youth. Both are asleep in the other
room with its door off the hinges, memories
of ourselves entwined with mythic lovers
in more perfect ways drifting in. Like Sullivan
we've toned the lyrics down. We are the sole
performers now and our skin wants nothing but
to stay on key and hold the memory of a gaze.

Beyond the Beatles Suite

JOHN LENNON AT THE DAKOTA

Funny, it's a knack I have,
something harder than to write a tune,
this right from wrong.
Still, that's what they'll say
I have to do. A boy needs shoes,
and a man needs blues.
Could be a line, or maybe two.
The studio's another day come soon.

So here we have it:
kindergarten.
Ladies, Gentlemen,
me work here's through.
I've taught him different
from the way me own da done.
To the playground, says I,
to the boathouse for snacks.
Just look across the park,
at the people lost in trees.

Look, how he comes
in pajamas and stocking feet.
And rubbin' his eyes
like the devil he is.
That's the way we mostly go:
in comfort, sleep in souls.
That's it, Boy, on me lap.
Today we sing these lullabies
widey, all widey awake.

PAUL MCCARTNEY'S COIN OF THE REALM

Paul McCartney's got a pocketed coin
he's been spending for three generations.

Paul McCartney's emerged from a dig,
complete in his regeneration.

Sir Paul bears a shield and a lance
on which sit the young generations.

Paul's taken troth of a bonnie lass born
of worship across generations.

McCartney's sued for the rights to songs
to generate wealth for the coming prince.

Survivor Paul plays benefits
for the fallen of all generations.

Paul McCartney's piano and hair
are immune to degeneration.

Ringo's the Gent Over There

We're on the set of *Caveman*,
on the cusp of another wife,
another odd career.

Ringo feels Hollywood's pull,
the pillow grip of a starlet's hand
on his furry forearm.

He also feels the beat
of Nineteen Sixty-Seven,
thinking this will never work.

No matter the effort
in dodging raptors,
nothing saves but a thump.

Encased in glass on Malibu Beach
he can't keep his hands from the tom
he beats in an empty room.

Ringo beats his tom
and beats his tom and
beats his tom,

rehearsing through remembrance
a short man's plan to see the world
high above the second half of life.

From the screen he is beating
a path back to fame
free of stardom's decay.

He will be what he has been
in the pantheon of sound:
The god who hides behind the kit.

George Harrison Died, Too.

The Buddhism might have saved him,
at least assured his energy in space.
Instead we have the riffs, some not his.

If he's weeping or wailing, we can't hear.
He's found his guru and better spouse in death.
As a wise man said, What else is there to do?

Think of him and John, the soulful ones.
Did they change the world like
Henry Ford and his naming of parts?

Jack White is some guitarist too, but really who cares?
From a rising Detroit a hundred Whites emerge
with misery their norm, in other words,

Has George found an end to suffering?
What is the sound of an endless progression
penned by someone bigger than Jesus Christ?

∞

Wolfman Jack and Everybody Else

A voice in the night has a face
the folks can't see but recognize.
This is the fact of the pact, the waves
from south of the border refracted
back atcha. Ain't no walls to block
the sounds of 1966, you dig?
Let me lay it down.

We gonna get to know each other
a little bit better, Baby.
We gonna take what we need
from the people and spit it
back at 'em, into space.
To all you comin' at me with ya wishes,
ya requests, all you campfire girls,
you choir boys, ringmasters,
and mistresses of the night,
I say, Don't stop, Don't stop.

This is the Wolfman callin'
to the traveling 50 thousand-watt
coast-to-coast circus,
all you hippies and PO-lice,
all you Tea-Partiers and Occupy types,
all you cable news junkies
tuned into your own thing,
my gracious, flow with the Wolfman,
flow back to that bedroom
where we all got close,
pull up those covers, dim those lights
and listen to one another in the dark,
how we used to. Shout if you want to,
tell everybody what you feelin'
but listen for the answers.

I'm way out here now, so I know
how an echo chamber feels.
I just keep laughing so I don't get lonely
talking to myself and no one sayin'

Stop, Stop, Wolfman, 'fore you drop.
How did they know what I know now?
Lemme tell ya, I see the future
from this great beyond. Boys and Girls,
once upon a time there was
this little kid in Brooklyn called Bob.
He wanted everybody loving him,
so he became the Wolfman.
But he had it wrong, you see.
Not everybody needs to love you.
That's what his mama and Wolfwoman do.

They burned crosses on my lawn
and I'm nothing but a black voice
inside a white man's hairy body.
That's what public love is worth.
But we got these airwaves,
and when they're singin',
you can't resist 'em.
You got the chance and you gotta
sell somethin' while you singin'.
That's all right for the Wolfman,
but the Wolfman's come and gone.
Somebody got to take his place.

The future's here, or it ain't.
The future's a roll call, and you be sure
you're in it, but you can't be there
by yourself. The future is all y'all back
inside the Wolfman's studio,
but it ain't the studio no more.
The studio ain't got no walls.
We can get ourselves naked, Baby,
without pretending like we don't see.
In Soul City nobody got on uniforms.
Nobody got on nothin'. We all be
little jaybirds singing our songs
at the Wolfman's pad, at the monster's ball.

Pass the malt liquor, pass the ideas,
drop your little egos in the car key jar.
Tune out those other voices
comin' at you from all those screens
and board rooms and back rooms
and bar rooms and green rooms.
Lift your radio to your shoulder.
Listen and listen and listen, and then
when your shoulder get tired,
you put that radio down,
and you ready to make the universe
a little less lonesome tonight.

When Gypsies Settle Down

The first time you heard them
        you might have found yourself in
Portugal or Ireland or Switzerland or
        Luxembourg, or maybe it was
France, though there's no way it was
        Germany, and years before you lived in
Italy, Bolivia, or Spain, when living meant
        not worrying how to live.

You were traveling because the world was
        traveling, people from different lands
making signs of the cross with their crossing paths,
        bowing on one another's soil,
placing open palms on foreign cities' cheeks,
        dancing across commons with polyglot partners,
whirling tatterdemalion of cultures
        finding music they could agree to share.

A band of Sevillano Gitanos found
        a lone rumbero from the West,
a story you made up because
        pesetas and francs, marks and escudos,
guilders and pounds, shillings and drachmas,
        lire were lyrics of forgotten Fascist songs,
marches replaced by the swing and sway
        of euros, "Bamboleo" and "Volare."

What irony that music of these gypsies
        springs from one specific place,
what luck that strife expelled it, drove them
        to Beijing, Bhagdad, Mumbai, Dakar,
the destinations of the opening world,
        what fortune to live inside a peace,
to hear that strum as a harmless storm,
        as vagabond with shelter anywhere.

What a dream to have known they were French,
        driven from Spain by part of a war
the world now used as abacus
        to calculate a future of exchange.
Exchange students took flamenco guitar
        and Saharan vocals for granted,
background music for televised falls: walls,
        taboos, dictatorships percussed.

This was the world the Gypsies feared to face,
        the one that birthed their fathers' sound,
the one you thought the villagers had burned,
        the villagers you thought were friends,
the friends who'd never hate again,
        the hatred driven out by minor chords,
the chords and wails divorced from oaths,
        the oaths you swore to this world.

But the world's rebuked the right to be
        gypsies, tunefully, in the olden ways,
appearing on late-night t.v. to plug
        soundtracks for Disney CGI,
for dancing not with you but with the stars,
        for agents in Beverly Hills,
playing engagements for travelers to Vegas
        afraid to hear this foreign music far from home.

Ledbetter

Hazy lyrics flow from a hazy mind,
so the snake is caught in the eaves.

Guitar gods sing as afterthought,
as narcissists blast their songs

while their victims sleep
instead of chatting to goodnight,

and a child downs the crumb cake
and wanders into Bolivian.

A near soldier unplugs his cable news
somewhere in SoCal

where the surf burns machines.
He befriends an Illinois kid

diving the waves for jam bands,
coming up with mouthfuls

of gargled lyrics and politics.
And the near soldier chooses

to surf the cove, not pound the Gulf.
But San Diego ain't L.A.,

where all the dreams are clowns.
He tries to stay home and love

his neighbors on the porch, but
they don't wave, don't even know

about his brother for his hair,
or the boxer for the bag,

or bigger bags stuffed with yellow
letters to tell you he died.

The oil coats the dooming birds
and both wash up on shore

like froths of boredom
that sounds like a season

when the surf kisses this guy
and the sun jigs sweet laments

he calls out to leave her
calm or gone or she goes or he

to follow Illinois to Seattle
to buy a deadbeat Louisiana.

MacArthur Park Covered Again

The benches have been beaten by the rain,
the iron of their armrests is exposed,
the wooden slats are splinters,
the checker tables crumbling
and the rusted barbecues.

The branches of the shade tree
are collapsing to the ground
near where the mud has claimed the pathways
and the feet we knew were walking
when the rain escaped the clouds.

The sweet green icing was pistachio
although the singers didn't taste it,
stricken as they were then
with love that left them desperate
on a paddle boat adrift.

They were shadowing the swans
when the warm wine and the hashish
seeped into their bones and goaded them
to drown their wails and sobs
someplace the lyrics hadn't named.

The baker tried his best
to recreate that cake, but couldn't
read the recipe he'd scribbled
on a napkin for his teardrops
when a Sunday soaked his dreams.

The ones who would've tried a slice
are older now, and those who get around
appear from time to time, to walk
and peer through leaves to catch
a sepia portrait of themselves

as Celtic bards in tights and scarves,
as Cowboys in striped pants and dancing
queens in fuchsia dresses, violinists
in black tie, emblazered crooners,
jazz quartets in silk brocade,

a comic in a bowler and a rayon
helmless spaceship captain
button-down philosopher,
and off-key red chanteuse
never sequined on a high.

They're waiting on the god of some
creation in a different song
as someone plays it low
on an abandoned radio
that dies a hero's death alone.

The Accuweather tells us
that the storm was never here and hit
another park where addicts spooned
their miners' shafts to cities
where no song had ever lived.

Composers no one's ever met
are sifting notes through strainers
in a country where the parks are fields
as parched as throats of lovers
hungry, woken by the sun.

Soon the sleeping singers rise
from caves of ice that gentrify
their minds with sins and dulcimers
confessed like crowds who lay
their lonely bedsheets on the grass.

Their private griefs now glitter
in the skyline like a galaxy
extinguished with the milk of
paradise baptizing victims
in a stream of yesterdays.

The voice that sings the part of rain
dissolves into the lightning
filling canyons with a metaphor
of decades meant for melody
and no one to explain.

I Believe the Children

The story doesn't mean the child kills
  the song. Instead a poor son
rest-stroke picked his way through jazz
  from Pittsburgh to Broadway to airwaves

faithful to anthem and oracle—
  one-time prodigy, legend, they said,
blessed with seven boys,
  none a bar to voice.

Of him we children knew
  just one melody we didn't need
to dream our future selves
  before children of our own.

We didn't see his dead sons' ghosts,
  who swaddled those transistored lines,
those wide lapels, those tortoiseshell frames
  televised on smoky stages.

All dramatic effect, the song
  asks us to believe in what
we used to be. All show biz
  sprouts from loamy platitudes.

Could he ask himself this?
  After funerals how much laughter
lives in the house of the living?
  The only choice was lying

to all of us soon to sleep and wake
  in lives before we understood
how they could have started. I believe
  we all move to the desert

where the artist leads us all
  to write unfinished songs of sins,
of loss of prince and princess,
  of future we can't claim for anyone.

Alec Baldwin's Ghost

I took my cousin to her senior prom: Massapequa, Long Island,
                                                      New York,
                 hometown of Alec Baldwin,
                       who must have been
                         homecoming king.

We went with her deformity   in lavender and gray.

I never once the whole night thought   of anything but how my hair stood up
and how embarrassed I felt   among someone else's
sometime friends.

Years later a friend told a story   of how Baldwin had returned
to their college, his alma mater,   how he'd sat in the commons,
                                                  waiting to be seen,
when my friend approached   the famous actor
and asked,
                       "Who are you?

Pink clouds slide across the clam shell sky
           like heartthrobs gone to seed   on a shimmering beach
                                                  we mortals can only dream.

                         Alec Baldwin used to summer here,
come back to live   nostalgic fantasy
on a seagrass shore   at curmudgeon ease
until driven by divorce   to hate the shape of life.

                        In his quest for peace,
I'd like to believe,   a higher power sent him back
                    to Massapequa
                        where
                    as I sit in my hometown
minivan parked on words   I should have spoken
with a younger tongue   on the road to Montauk

                    as he ponders his next move
                    in the kitchen of a Cape
I'd like to believe   his family's never sold,

I'd prefer not to be,
in this early hour   of sunset success

            Alec Baldwin's ghost.

The Awkward Outrage of Fred Goldman

        Red lights atop cameras,
THIS MAN, he cried, and nothing ever more,
            the man whose lush mane of coiffed mottle
            spoke tomes of justice.

      Months he played the God of Outrage,
           hurling awkward   silence cloaked in tweed
        at proselytes of telelegal drama.
A man of neither word nor gesture,
        his magnified eyes damned microphones to hell.

No one will ever burn
        Fred Goldman in effigy:
                  victim's victim,
a man who'd lost the life of life
        to someone else's anger.

        Like the parents   of Nicole and O. J.

     But this is years ago and you
              will not remember these names.
Like all the parents   of killers and victims,
         we all still need a name
                not O. J.
The hero may have killed, but the name cannot
                  mean killer.
          a name like Marsha Clark,
        or bloody glove
         or White Bronco

                The idea of justice
                needs a void
                like Goldman's silence.

        Years hence we fumble

        Embroiled in right and wrong,
        in accidents of race,
        in gorgeous bodies daring sex and death,
        and in attorney's rhymes.

We lost Fred Goldman   in the flashbulb's pop.

                another man a memory,
                as he
                        by luminous infinity pool
        wonders why
                        the world ever had his silence.

The Idiosyncrasy of Otis Redding

He almost trips
over notes. He's talking
to himself through
Dixie cups and string,
she said. He
sounds
like a man
who's been strung out
so long
he can't stop
staring at
the sea.
If you ask me,
what he sang
wasn't soul at all.
And "Tenderness,"
it's not tender,
pure pain.
And why
are all the greats in pain?
Do you hear
how he steals
harmony on
"Bring It On Home."
A thief.
Now
wait a minute.
Listen
to the way
he steps. A signal
for a kiss, but
no.
He's making love
to the mic.

Rough love. Almost
Ike and Tina love.
These songs connect
him. Each is
someone else
he knew.
He liked it best
alone.
You hear that,
don't you?
He wants you to
know what it is
to be
alone.
(As she breaks my heart.)
That's it,
what makes him
strange. He's singing
to heartbreak, like
he'll never find it,
never feel it.
It's autistic
soul. His voice is
his own
therapy.
Do you know?
Did he die
alone?

I thought.
I nodded.
I hummed
to myself.

Being Stevie Wonder

GROOVE

π

LOVE

VISION

POLY

*

ﷺ

SOUL

HIGHER

FINGERTIPS

You hear that?

Zen of Bruce Lee

                        I does not exist
                                exit
                        the namesake
                        forever returning
                        high-pitched while whirling   tiger
                        stoic tai chi in buffchest   dancer
                        trembling electric current weapon
                        he could turn on himself before
                                      dying of a curse,
                        of allergy to pain
                        killers, of hospitals, halls
                        he never walked fearless
                        as the downward glare
                        a dozen fighters closing in
                        like Hollywood truth
                        the master who beat him
                        privately women kept him
                        from children from names
                        Lee Jun-fan Lee Sai-fon
                        Lee Yuen-cham Lee Siu-lung
                        allowing him to breathe
                        required bodies not forged
                        in the fire of will destroy
                        the image is the only
                        directive he failed
                        to execute
                        child of opera poet
                philosopher college student
          Hong Kong street fighter
     American teacher style of no
         style   shape shapeless as water
         actor again   when image swelled
         choreographer   beyond control beyond
         Manson murder   mythology beyond
         suspect   mind bending body
invisible neurotic   to will its opposite
                        opposite of
                        zen brain swollen
                        proof elusive
                        as fists as
                        reason
                        he still
                        exists as I

A Fool Believes

A fool believes in music
as a pre-teen walks
for a distant cancer cure
on a spring day in 1980.
A gaggle of fools follows
the beat of the Doobies
along the dubious course.

I'd rather be a fool
who believes his father
will never get sick or die,
who walks for a cure
to all the pain he knows
he'll never feel, who believes
in Michael McDonald's voice
and knows wise men
have no power to reason
lyrics or fears away.

No song will ever be so
popular. No song will ever
knock it from its perch.
Casey Kasem means it
when he calls it historic.
If my father just listened
all the way through,
long enough to lose track
of his time on earth,
he'd understand the music,
what it makes us, and not only
what a fool believes, but why.

Winter 1944

John Wayne had black hair
the first time you saw him
for five cents and a walk
through deep snow you knew
like lines from *The Fighting
Kentuckians,* people who climbed hills
to reach their kin, shooting homemade
slingshots, dragging broomstick
horses through the dust.
For a nickel. I wish I could
have watched them at your side
but then I would not have this
father to tell me how it was.

What Seems Still Whirls

Fifteen, aboard a flight to Spain,
Twilight Zone: The Movie
fresh in mind, its demons
not yet on the wing, not yet.
Still, any view is of fear.
Fifty-one on a parlor couch,
finished with *The Blackboard Jungle*
Vic Morrow as a high school hood,
I ponder the terrors of turbulence
in swirling winds, the turbulence
of teenage love abroad or else
at home, the kind of love that West
(Morrow's delinquent) never knows.
Take your hat off in class, Mr. Dadier
(Daddy-O), his teacher, commands,
West's hair a whorl of chaos.
But West gets his revenge
in alleyway fisticuffs.
Coincidence that *Combat*, t.v. drama,
will be Morrow's transport
into every living room,
his dark day in the sun.
Morrow, a good stage name
for a tough Jewish kid,
a genuine Stanley Kowalski,
Morrow, grown believer now
sending t.v. Nazis down.

My first flight to Europe,
my seat aboard the boomerang.
Turbulence. No comfort in props,
the literalist's flight,
only my classmates familiar.
Morrow knew Elvis and Curtiz,
who directed *Casablanca*.
The fascists lost the fight
and only a Clash song
spun them back. Morrow was born
a villain like us all. Born to live,
to strut, to suffer, die and live

again in children, actors acting
in our places. Morrow's daughter
suffered too the wounds
that open every day.

How could I know how many times
I'd cross the pond on missions
secret to me as everyone else?
Different mines each time:
Friends, lovers, parents
blown up in a field,
in a peasant border village,
in historic spirals,
rotation of ages, faces,
feelings come back to steal
consciousness of moments.
Each time a hill to take and then
another, machine guns spinning
bullets into close relations.

A landscape like Vietnam.
The director showed Morrow in stills
how Indian Dunes could substitute.
It had so many times. The site of
bikes grooving circles in sand,
dunes shifting with nearby tides,
and Magic Mountain Amusement Park,
the kid's vacation giving way
to overseas flights and nights
on Spanish beaches, stirring sangria
that back home would have made us
Wests, the post-War city toughs, the gangs
that ruled the roost, the dynamos
of matching jackets, blades flashing
through the air, ballet
scored by Bernstein, circling back
a decade later to radical chic,
a new generation of sons at war,
fathers from the G. I. Bill,
Daddy-Os like my own

who threaded a needle between
the law and war, becoming cops,
firemen, accountants, clerks,
spinning us out to suburbs, spinning
off families whose mission it was
to learn what our parents denied:
What seems still whirls

I was a straight-A first-date student—
the first like the hundredth—
to see that *Twilight Zone*,
with Morrow cast as cynic
a-whirl through time, the Zone
with its animated whorl
to a fifth dimension
beyond sight and sound,
superstition and science,
the opposite of amnesia,
where Serling could have plucked him
from an eddy of actors,
but instead, a generation out
the movie took him for good.
The heat of fake explosions,
delaminated rotors
whirling downward
decapitating Morrow,
knocking the orb of life
from its path, and with it
children he meant to redeem.

I am here to watch the credits roll,
Daddy-O now, confused about
this scene, my shoulders slumped,
no longer moving freely through the set
the world becomes, the stir of faces,
ages gone, the whirl of the done,
so that, in Morrow's final words,
I've got to be crazy to do this shot.
I should've asked for a double.

Boom!

If we are allegory,
we must drink ourselves
almost to the point of shouts
at the Angel of Death, who comes
when scarcely older than La Taylor
on that majestic set, where white backs
to his black, we think, *Injection!*

If we live for ages,
we must live on celluloid
and die in an Elysée
around the corner from Modern Art's
retrospective of our later years
filled with times together
screaming, *Urgentissimo!*

If we are poets, we must come
as Witches of Capri,
Hepburns in Cowards' clothes, who
like fathers with poor business plans,
wish the still living dead,
as in Kibukimono they
declare, *Goforth!*

If our careers continue, we
prolong the fatal binge
in a screenplay of medusas
and silent hallelujahs sung
by intercom to stern auteurs
musing upon the stagey waves,
and cry out, *Oh, wine-dark sea!*

The Colonel Dreams Equestrian Elvis

Whoa, Colonel Midnight!
Whoa there, Boy!

I can smell the leather of his saddle.
Feel the spurs poke me gentle
in the Mississippi mist.
We're alone, together,
the two of us again.
I carry him toward the river
like another Robert E. Lee.
He twirls the whip
but doesn't use it.
I hide my true accent.

Easy now.

I'd do anything for that voice.
Leap a hedge
Let his friend's wife ride me.
Stand next to the palomino
for a home movie.

Git along, Big Fella.

I make him bigger than life,
carry him across the world.
He's hero for us both,
a resurrected cavalry of two.
He snaps the reins.
I gallop toward a gala in the distance.
The heavens spotlight
Priscilla on a pedestal.
He catches sight,
twists my head away.
I whinny.
Cameras roll across the meadow,
mounted on golden Cadillacs
the way I've planned it.

Well, don't that beat all.

He tugs me to a stop.
I turn and show him
my most heartfelt eye,
a look that pleads to please
don't sell me off.

*I guess we oughtta do it, Hoss.
It's what the people want.*

I know he'll listen,
because my cut is fair,
because I keep the river's pace
like we were natives to a carnival
called America,
because neither of us bucks,
because, at any time, I let him know,
we can disappear into the hills.

Elvis Costello in the Bargain Bin

The kids don't understand.
Diana Krall throws up her hands.
They don't know why he wakes at 3 a. m.
to walk the hall, Valhalla-bound,
to a padded room, to keyboard chords
and harmonies that want
a trial, so he judges them,
directs himself through breakfast,
smiles too much and riffles
clefs for promises. Half sold-out,
half-resistant, as songs keep
pouring, then evaporate
dry as antiperspirant.

These days we all wish
we could write good tunes. Back then
we'd rather have slung guitars,
been blokes in tight black suits, so bitter
no girl could want us. Coolest was
the knock-kneed cardboard cut-out
peering over jumbo shades
down the record aisle at Sears.
We, grown enough to laugh and cry,
understood that trust was just a song
without words, insecurity
with a backbeat, big bass line,
wild organ runs, slashing riffs,
voice deep enough to roar
disgust, amusement, angelic contempt.

No matter how long he played
with others, he was never part
of a band. He was only himself,
expanding, contracting
signing on dotted lines,
marking quarter rests
that disappeared so fast
even Paul McCartney couldn't
rediscover the ineffable tone,
no matter how thin he stayed.

This current Elvis grows
from constant composition, dynamite,
because this world will never need
an endless stream of notes
and ideas from a man out of time
who slips into jazz and New York
with his New World wife
by a plan he wrote in youth,

while we were tuning in to learn
that we could ape the horn-rimmed nerd,
the mysteries belonged to him,
the him we couldn't know,
the man who'd end in box store
bargain bins, where he belongs
to us again. We guess he knows
as much as anyone can of a gift
as we struggle to impress
our kings and queens, to pay
our bills, to keep our jobs
and find creative outlets
for our grief, to find the formula
for life as long as expectation,
but, hiding in his vest and porkpie hat
and two day's growth, he can't explain
why clever lyrics matter,
or a sharp hook,
or the lack.

José Feliciano's National Anthem

You want people to pay attention, but they so rarely do.
So José had to sing and sing and sing.

At the '68 World Series. Lolich versus Hoerner.
No one remembers the match-up.

Everyone remembers the anthem.
José sang it with soul, sang to you.

He always sang to you, no matter how many
yous there were. Whether or not you were there.

You are Mickey Lolich, warming in the bullpen
and your team is down three games to one,

and Detroit is down, and your country is down,
and you are twenty-eight years old, five years

José's senior, and will pitch eleven more
and stay alive his entire career, but for now

you try your slider to a strange familiar tune
over the P. A. and as many boos as cheers.

A crowd is a cruel and merciful thing.
José's career will never be the same,

how the tricycle accident changed you from righty
to lefty, but only in that act

that's made you famous and sometimes
beloved. (You'd lose almost as many as you'd win.)

You wish you could hear him sing again, and will.

He will sing on the news that night, and suffer,
and always find another place to play.

Behind the Iron Curtain. On Sesame Street.
On *Chico and the Man*. With the Vienna Symphony.

Decades later, in the movie *Fargo*, mocked:
José Feliciano, you got no complaints.

And yet, and yet, and yet he sings,
because you need him to. Because when they ask

he says he just wanted people to notice
the song, because this country gives you a chance

even if the country, like music, eludes him,
escapes us, leaves us needing it, the way

the '68 Cardinals couldn't hold on,
could only keep playing through coming years

of national anthems and more losses than wins
until they could hear him sing again, sing

Just let go, and you'll get all the music you need.

Eubie's Rag

He's shrunk to the size of a black silk vest, to the size of eyes
behind bottle-bottom glasses, the size of a steady left hand.

Ancient fingers prance across black keys like a century.
Not quite a century, but why should we assume Gerontion?

To disappear this way, all you have to do is age to ripeness,
age to rediscovery, keep a time that folks forget.

To get on television, you live just long enough to play the unfamiliar,
tell stories of rhythm's name, and become a banded bowler hat.

You claim that once when living in old Baltimore
you met a man who told you cakewalk, prizewalk, thump,

and that's all that you remember, except how light or heavy
the rag could be, how sweet it felt to play the tune.

Years later you write it down because ears steal,
because you can write, because you plan to stay alive.

And don't ever say you're only ninety-nine
when the people would rather clap to a hundred.

Music is the oldest story going, so once in a hundred years
we let an old man tell it from the top, as if he knew.

Louis Prima at the Carousel Bar

The dyed black hair of his bowed crown,
and down the bar the double of his ex.

I don't ask. He says. After a set, the carousel
inches us along a stretch of Royal Street.

Like all the secrets of another year.
He wonders aloud where he'd be.

Where he should if he hadn't gone
for the riff as much a joke as *Hey*,

*you heard the one about the judge
wore a corset underneath his robe?*

    What music you know as a kid?
    He asks. Beatles. Don't matter. For him:

    "Just a Gigolo" "I Ain't Got Nobody"
    "Sheik of Araby" That kinda tune.

    He says. Gimme bourbon neat. Old Crow.
    Gimme another chance. Gimme Gimme.

    That'd be some kind of song. See.
    Even now. See the way it's…What's the word?

      Irresistible. Like a pretty girl
      in a cocktail dress. *Salut'* to the barmaid.

        Know what they say about your health?
        A pill with whiskey. A wink. He asks.

        You want I sing you something?
        Tells me. Best tune's like a summer's day.

        You can sing it, but you don't have to.
        To enjoy. Wrote a few. Six, seven chords.

        Coulda written more. Lot more. But
        loneliness gets you. Tall grass. You

sitting there by yourself in a room
trying to rest on the quiet in your head.

    That's always there, and you try to ignore.
    Too much quiet in the world. Talk to me,

        Brother. Tell me what I oughtta play.
        It's better than art. Belts the bourbon.

        Though they say. He says. Art lasts
        longer than a kiss. See that girl.

            The bar comes around. Think she'll kiss me
            if I blow my horn the way she likes to hear?

Nothing But Love Songs

If loving you is wrong
I don't want to be right
cause it's the right time of the night
for makin' love.
I feel like makin' love,
though I know love stinks,
smells like teen spirit,
but I'm going up
to the spirit in the sky,
where all the leaves are brown
with a touch of gray saying
touch me in the morning,
then just go away,
go away little girl,
my girl, my best friend's girl,
the kind of girl you want so much
it makes you sorry.
Please accept my apology.
Please, please me.
Please, Baby, Please,
don't go breakin' my heart.
Please don't go.
If you go, don't look back.
Get back.
Where have all the good times gone?
Let the good times roll.
Let 'em roll, Baby, roll,
all night long.
You shook me
all night long.
I ain't even done with the night,
even if you done me wrong.
Must've been that time
was never on my side.

A Mother Explains the Lyrics

Trenchtown. It's in Jamaica.
The government's terrible.
The people suffer.
Nobody cares.
But they're happy,
because they sing.
They love to sing.
He's thinking about it.

This song's about the South.
And his family.
The society has problems,
but it's still home.
Mussel Shoals is another town.
The government's corrupt there
too, in Alabama.
But they like the Governor
because northerners hate him.
You know how they are.
Still fighting the Civil War.

Bobbie McGee was a woman he loved,
but she left him,
because no woman wants to stay poor.
Looks are nice,
but a woman won't stay for that alone,
unless you can sell your songs.
I can't tell you what it means
when a woman sings it.

He thinks they were born to run,
that that's the way to stay young.
You can't stay young.
Why would you want to?
Young people are melodramatic
about sadness and motorcycles.
If you ride either one too long,
you're bound to have an accident.

He's singing about how he wants to go home,
to Australia.
They have toads with horns on their backs.
He hunted them when he was young.
And he must have seen *The Wizard of Oz*.
But he was the opposite of Dorothy.
He wanted to get away.
So he got on the yellow brick road.
But he should have stayed in the country.

It's not that he doesn't like September.
It's a metaphor.
For 9-11
Maybe you were too young.
You were innocent.
Like he says he was.
Though when it comes to things like that,
you were only innocent
if you weren't paying attention.

Da-Doo-Doo-Doo, like a baby.
The singer has nothing to say,
so he thinks if he says nothing
people will think he's innocent.
But he can't be. He knows
enough to keep his mouth shut,
at least while he's singing.

She's saying she's not really a virgin,
but that anyone can be surprised
if she puts her mind to it.
When it comes to music
we're all virgins
when a song touches us
for the first time.
It's a nice thought,
but why does she have to be so crude?

Zen of Iggy Pop

                                                          Fuck you, Miami Beach
                                                          Fuck you, U S of A

I'm swimming to my shanty town
I'm swimming to my shanty town   and the joke is on the blues
I'm swimming to my shanty town

                                                the joke is on consumers of

    You are
            these shards
                        You are
                                  these grooves
                                            these lacerations

      And I
              am Elvis
                    crucified

                                And I
                                    will not
                                              be captured

                              And we

                              will

                              unlearn

                              yesterday

                                          Ha Ha Ha
              Ha Ha   Ha HA

            Let us outlive history, the dabbling in, the sinew of
                                      the night of
                      this iguana
                              unfathomable plot

                                        no plot

                        except a Midwest gentleman
                        waltzing—more like prancing—
                        is you the moment you wake
                        from your most upsetting dream
                        is the smile playing on your lips
                        to think you've woken up at all

            and, oh, oh, yeah

                            you millions
                              you prizes
                                you hypnotized

    flesh machine chickens

in your split-level vinyl-stocked listening rooms,

                Hey
                                Yeah
                                                Fuck you too

ABOUT THE AUTHOR

George Guida is the author of eight books, including four previous collections of poems. He serves as Senior Advisory Editor for *2 Bridges Review*, and teaches writing, literature, and cultural studies at New York City College of Technology. With his wife he owns the MacFadden Coffee Company, a music and poetry café in Dansville, New York.

www.ingramcontent.com/pod-product-compliance
Lightning Source LLC
Chambersburg PA
CBHW030157100526
44592CB00009B/319